SEGREGATED CLASS PLACEMENT VS HETEROGENEOUS CLASS

PLACEMENT OF EMOTIONALLY AND PERCEPTUALLY

HANDICAPPED CHILDREN

A Dissertation

Utah State University

Doctor of Education in Educational Psychology

by

Ronald Ora John

1967

Reprinted in 1975 by

R AND E RESEARCH ASSOCIATES
4843 Mission Street, San Francisco 94112
18581 McFarland Avenue, Saratoga, California 95070

Publishers and Distributors of Ethnic Studies
Editor: Adam S. Eterovich
Publisher: Robert D. Reed

Library of Congress Card Catalog Number

74-29575

ISBN

0-88247-315-8

TABLE OF CONTENTS

LIST OF TABLES

ACKNOWLEDGEMENTS

I wish to express my appreciation to Dr. Ronald Peterson, Dr. Stephen White, Dr. Glendon Casto and Mr. Richard Enos for their trust in my competency to earn the degree, and to my son, Cameron R. John, whose acceptance of my absence and open devotion added impetus to my desire to finish.

Ronald Ora John

INTRODUCTION

Good education and good curriculum planning make use of available processes, techniques, and knowledge in providing for the needs of children over a broad range of capacities and performance. In recent years increased attention has been given to planning for the education of children with characteristics placing them far enough from the norm to be labeled "atypical". However, after placing children in existing programs of special education, there still remained a group with learning and behavioral problems of sufficient intensity to merit additional attention. Some children remaining in this group showed indications of neurological handicaps (sometimes called perceptual handicaps, perceptual dysfunction, central nervous system dysfunction, etc.), and others given indications of a primary emotional handicap. These children had severe learning problems even though they have dull normal to above mental ability as measured by common psychometric devices.

In general, programs for the above two categories of children have been considered to require such distinct provisions that the two kinds of children must be kept separate. This development may be due to basic differences in needs, but it is also possible that a tendency to concentrate on differences has led to a neglect of the similarities of needs. Perhaps an increased concern in this area by general curriculum planners would complement the intensive and extended concern by specialists.

Poudre R-1 School District of Fort Collins, Colorado, has
started a program as a result of a federal grant (PL 89-10) under Title
III which provides for the education of neurologically handicapped children and emotionally handicapped children under an "umbrella program".
Such a combination has not been educationally attempted previously as
part of a Colorado state-wide public school program. A comprehensive
review of other states' public school programs gave evidence that there
did not exist a program in the United States where the type of grouping
done by Poudre School District was being attempted or researched.

The purpose of this study was to evaluate the effectiveness
of three different classroom settings for children identified as perceptually and/or emotionally handicapped. These settings consisted of (1)
regular school placement of these children with no designed manipulation
of his class environment, (2) A half day placement in a regular class
and the other half day spent in a segregated class setting designed for
remediation of the student's particular difficulties, (3) A full day
setting where six of these children were placed in a classroom with
eighteen regular children. A second specialist teacher was added to this
classroom to deal primarily with the needs of these children.

Evaluative criterion was of changes on tests of intelligence,
achievement, perceptual organization and self concept.

REVIEW OF LITERATURE

Any consideration for programming for emotionally disturbed
or educationally handicapped children must take into consideration a
few historical highlights in order to provide sufficient background to
appreciate and understand the present state of development. In review-
ing the literature, it was decided to consider the significant studies
and reports in two areas:

1. The area of programs for children with cerebral dysfunction.

2. The philosophy and setting of emotionally disturbed pro-
    grams for children in public schools

Programs for Children with Cerebral Dysfunction

Mahler (1964) presented an excellent review of literature in the
area of cerebral dysfunction which is summarized as part of the review.
Interest in the possible effects of brain damage on learning can be
traced back as far as 1819 when Gall, a Viennese physician, described two
cases of loss of language function after head injury (right hemiplegia)
and suggested speech functions were localized in the anterior areas of
the brain. Broca (1861) reported two cases of "amphemia" (articulated
language disorder) and outlined the destruction which he had found at
necropsy, later reporting on eighteen more cases. He firmly believed the
left half of the brain was the center of language function, and his finding of 19 lesions in the third front gyrus of the left hemisphere in 20

necropsies on adults who had suffered a loss of speech provokes considerable opposition and continuing discussion. Trousseau in 1864 introduced the term "aphasia," (after learning the term "speechlessness" was used before the days of Christ) in use today--one hundred years later--and still being debated in terms of its actual existence.

The year 1864 also marked the beginning of reports by Hughlings Jackson (1932), a British physician, on his observations on speech function and loss. For the next thirty years, until 1893, he continued his precise clinical observations that gradually evolved into his theories of language and cerebral functioning. The contemporary approach in Jackson's day was structural (organic) and Jackson's analysis could only be grasped in terms of a functional concept of behavior. For at least fifty years (Weisenburg, 1935) much of his work was neglected or ignored, possibly because others lacked his grasp of the complexity of cerebral functioning. However others did explore the approach he presented and in turn made, and continue to make, substantial contributions to our understanding of cerebral and nervous functioning.

Head (1915) reported that Jackson differentiated asphasia into two main groups: Those who were speechless or whose speech was very much damaged and those whose speech was plentiful but disturbed by many errors (in a more precise term for the second group might be dysphasia). His most significant findings and theories are summarized as follows:

1. The realization that destructive injury does not cause

positive effects but instead induces negative conditions which allow
positive symptoms to appear.

2. The observation of automatic or emotional speech even when
voluntary speech was absent.

3. The learning and storage and recall of automatic speech
is conducted in both hemispheres of the brain, while propositional
speech (a higher functional level) is primarily seated in one dominant
hemisphere (the left).

4. Likewise his conclusion that damage to but one hemisphere
can render a man speechless.

5. His appreciation of the impossibility of limiting the problem to a dichotomy of speech or intelligence--considering it instead a
complex mixture of degrees and kinds of involvement of the whole brain
or even the whole body.

6. His discovery of visual-perceptual dysfunction as distinct
from word-perceptual dysfunction, which he labeled "imperception"--thus
the forerunner of the contemporary term "agnosia".

The only criticism of Jackson's observations seems to have been
from his contemporaries over his failure to accept the the then current
brain-lesion specific-area explanation from aphasia.

Aphasia has continued to be a fascinating, and often stormy,
topic right up until the present day, attracting the interest of workers
as far apart as Japan and Sweden (Malmquist 1958). It is notable that

far more work seems to have been done on aphasia in Europe and in Great Britain then in the United States until after World War II, when military injuries spurred research in the subject.

Although he is now largely known for his later work in psychoanalysis, the neurologist Sigmund Freud wrote an excellent book On Aphasia (1891) which followed Jackson's views on functional development. Indeed Freud criticized virtually every other worker but Jackson and stated he was adopting Jackson's views on levels of functioning and retrogression. Freud's book supplies the transition between his works on neurology and personality and clearly indicated the genesis of much of his theories of projection, representation, memories, suppression, and speech slips--"Freudian slips". Freud himself continued to regard this work as valuable (Freud, 1950) but it has been virtually unknown in Britain and America.

The expansion of interest in aphasia and the rapid expansion of education next combined to stimulate a concern for the pronounced learning disability--the apparent inability (alexia) or gross difficulty (dyslexia) in perceiving or understanding letter or work forms, existing apart from other disturbances. Another British physician, James Hinshelwood (1917), is considered by many, including Gates (1947) to have presented outstanding work in favor of the view that reading difficulty is due to organic defects. From an early period many efforts were made to link reading difficulties to defects in the receptive organs (eyes, ears), in the excessive organs (such as the tongue), the expressive mechanisms (such as speech) and the like, but Hinshelwood proposed the hypothesis that children who were unable to learn to read but who presented no difficulty in visual acuity were "congenitally word-blind" owing to the failure of certain localized areas of the brain to develop their particular functions. He attributed a lack of visual memory to defective development of an area of the brain called the angular gyrus, thought at that time to be the storehouse of visual memories of words. Henshelwood developed this theory from his careful work over twenty years with persons with severe reading disabilities, including those who lost the ability to read as the result of injuries to localized areas of the brain, and these cases he labeled "acquired word-blindness". He emphasized the seriousness of the defect, the cause as a pathological condition, and that the condition was not complicated by other signs of cerebral defect or visual disorders. He further stated that general intelligence, powers of observation, reasoning, and auditory memory are not affected in cases of true word-blindness. This definition and his meticulous descriptions have been widely accepted and adopted under the heading of "congenital dyslexia". Except for minor changes, his work forms the basis for much contemporary thinking about brain-defects as a cause of dyslexia.

Hinshelwood's theory has never been fully tested because methods of verification have not yet been established (Robinson, 1946).

However, much empirical evidence has come from agencies dealing with long-term consequences of trauma, such as the U.S. Veterans' Administration hospitals since World War II (John Money, 1963).

Smith and Carrigan (1959) paid tribute to Hinshelwood but state his theory is deficient in that it fails to account for the factors they feel important, such as blending deficiency, slow reading rate, and deficient discrimination. They proposed a Theory of Synoptic Transmission to explain the same behavior.

Gates (1947), while acknowledging Hinshelwood's work, declined to accept the concept of a clear syndrome, capable of being labeled word-blind-ness (apparently believing disabilities tend to involve more than one area and to be functional in cause).

Regardless of the continuing controversy over one or more aspects of alexia and dyslexia, Hinshelwood's (1917) contributions are substantial for at least the following reasons:

1. His systematic observations of children and adults with severe reading disabilities but normal intelligence, covering a 20-year period, firmly established the concept of cerebral dysfunction as one cause of reading failure.

2. His clinical observations and autopsies stimulated great effort in understanding neuro-psychology.

3. He provided definitions and diagnostic symptomatology which are still models for studies.

4. He gave us the term "word-blindness" which has now become

an integral part of the jargon of education and neurology.

The next consideration should be directed to a physician in the United States, the eminent neuro-pathologist Samuel T. Orton. Dr. Orton in his famous paper in which he proposed the term "strephosymbolia" (Orton, 1928) (literally "twisted symbols") stated that the evidence "must be held to militate against the hypothesis of a congenital brain defect" (page 1096). He began his work with fifteen children but later was able to conduct a two year study, with the aid of the Rockefeller Foundation, on 175 reading disabled children and 120 normal readers. From this he developed certain basic concepts:

1. Strephosymbolia forms a clear-cut clinical entity which can be diagnosed by appropriate methods.

2. It is not related to feeblemindedness and may occur at any intellectual level.

3. It is due to a variant in the establishment of the physiologic lead in the hemispheres rather than a pathological condition.

4. The cases form a series graded in severity from mild to the extreme.

5. At least 2 per cent of the school population has this defect.

6. Re-education methods should be based on training for simultaneous association of visual, auditory, and kinesthetic fields, with prognosis good if started early and continued conscientiously.

7. The consequences of the disability often cause significant

emotional problems which then tend to further impede school progress.

Dr. Orton continued to be active in neurology, reading, and psychiatry until his accidental death in 1948. He has left behind the very active Orton Society (continuing to support studies and publish work on cerebral dysfunctioning; several schools, important publications, and a host of co-workers who have made significant contributions. One of these was Marion Monroe who worked with him on his first large study and reported it in 1928, following it with another extensive study reported in 1932 which is still a significant study of the multiple factors which impede reading, as well as a storehouse for remedial methods. Another was Lauretta Bender whose work in developing the Bender Gestalt test is more well known but no more important than the work on problems in conceptualizations and communication--work begun with Dr. Orton in 1926. And another, Mrs. De Hirsch, was recently interviewed in a serious work on dyslexia in "The New Yorker" (September 14, 1963), in which she suggested about 7 per cent of all children suffer from reading, writing and spelling dyslexia.

Saunders (1962) gave Orton credit for his pioneering work in describing and defining the dyslexia syndrome in the United States and for his contributions in inspiring the development of effective educational techniques.

Smith and Carrigan (1959) believed the dominance theory of Orton "is of little apparent utility" and his technique is unrelated to his theory. They suggested that studies on incidence of dominance problems in remedial cases tend to reflect the biases of the investigators. Delacato (1961) advocated a program of making the child completely unilateral and establishing complete sequential organization as the basis for treating severe reading problems and as such seemed to be supporting Orton.

Joe Eisenson (1958) supported the position of Orton and Bender in stating "My own inclination is to think in terms of a maturational delay or an atypical development of the language centers rather than of a specific lesion," (this could include factors affecting both speech and reading).

Gates (1947b) stated that "The idea of word recognition being due to impressions stored up as copies or images or as engrams literally etched in one hemisphere in one form and in the other in mirrored form is unacceptable to most psychologists. Finally, data gathered on the frequency of cases showing lack of hand dominance--suggested by Orton as a test of brain dominance--do not confirm the theory."[1]

Concern for atypical children is generated by concern over the inefficiency and inappropriateness of much of their behavior, and this quite naturally leads to an ultimate concern for learning problems and their solutions. In the United States, Strauss and Lehtinen (1947) are almost universally given credit for initiating extensive and expanding interest in all aspects of the brain-damaged child. A physician and a teacher, Strauss and Lehtinen, worked with brain damaged children for over 20 years, using both private and public school facilities, before

11

publishing their first book.

The investigators concluded from their many cases that brain-injury results in perceptual disturbances, and then designed a marble-board test, a tachistoschopically presented visual-perception test, a hidden tactual-motor test, and an auditory-perception test to examine their hypothesis. Extended testing with numerous children, normal, retarded, and brain-injured, led to the conclusion that perceptual disturbances belong to a characteristic motor-perceptual syndrome which can be observed to exist in the visual, the factual, and the auditory field--all based upon a defective figure--ground relation.

Investigations were also conducted demonstrating the increased perseveration of brain-injured children, using tone patterns, line drawings, and dotted cards. Concept formation was examined with classification (sorting) tests and with picture-object tests. The findings indicated "brain-injured children, as compared with non-brain-injured normal and mentally deficient children, selected more objects, made more uncommon choices, "went-off" more easily to elaborate on conceptual units only loosely connected with the task at hand, and exhibited pedantic and formalistic behavior in arrangement of objects."

Behavior disorders which seemed to stem from organic factors were examined and compared with the behavior of emotionally disturbed non-organic children, using clinical evaluations and behavior rating scales. Results indicated significant differences in many areas, such as excessive motor activity, and emphasized the difficulty of effective treatment of many behavior disorders.

The total findings of Strauss and Lehtinen were applied to an educational schema designed to: (1) manipulate and control the external over-stimulating environment, and (2) educate the child to the exercise of voluntary control. This involved small class (not more than 12 pupils), minimal room decorations, arrangement of furniture conducive to undistracted study, and teaching methods and materials designed to un-distracted study, and teaching methods and materials designed to present only the essential elements of a process, while including purposeful motor activity whenever possible. A caution is included that materials should not be themselves regarded as methods, and that both require extensive modifications because of the extreme differences in individual needs. An important point often overlooked, is that special class placement is not a substitute for a regular program; it is an interim provision until the child can return to a more appropriate program, with or without part time supportive help.

The contributions of Strauss and Lehtinen cannot adequately be summarized, but these four are perhaps most important to school personnel:

1. Developed a general theory of figure-ground deficiency to account for the erratic behavior of brain-injured children.

2. Developed tests and methods to identify such deficiency.

3. Developed educational methods designed to strengthen figure-ground perception.

13

4. Stimulated extensive continuing research.

Negative criticism of Strauss tends to center around the lack of information of the numbers of children worked within various aspects of his study and the lack of statistical controls. Positive comments are infinitely more numerous, especially for the scope of the illumination directed upon the problem. Both positions are well summarized by Cruickshank (1961).

A subsequent volume by Strauss and Kephart (1955) continued with modifications for diagnosing and educating the brain-injured child. Original concepts were broadened to more nearly include the child with normal all-over ability and emphasizes the involvement of the total nervous and motor system in thinking and in behavior. The authors (p. 143) suggest that difficulties "are primarily a result of interference with the patterning activity of the brain; that they result from interference, not with specific functions, but with more generalized functions concerned with the development of patterns of excitation."

Extensive material was presented on developments in neurology, followed by benchmark sections devoted to language, thinking, and concept formation.

A widely discussed study was conducted in Maryland with the aid of the Federal Government and reported by Cruickshank (1961, p. 25). Called by the investigators a pilot study, its two chief aims were:

   1. In terms of their appropriateness to the instructional
      and social needs of hyperactive, emotionally disturbed
      children with or without evidence of brain injury, to

14

investigate and evaluate the usefulness of teaching
methods developed in an experimental setting for brain-
injured children.

2. To carry out the pilot study within the framework of
the administrative policies and procedures of a public
school system.

The study concerned itself with forty children who were educationally retarded, between the ages of 6-11 and 10-11 with I.Q. scores
on the Stanford-Binet between 51 and 107. Extensive medical and psychological diagnostic procedures selected children which were divided into
four classes of ten children each, half the children in each class did
not have a brain-injury diagnosis. Two classes were operated under
carefully structured conditions, using a modified Strauss-Lehtinen approach, while the other two were control groups with teachers left free
to work on their own. The two demonstration classes also had teaching
assistants and a speech therapist available. The demonstration classes
followed a program based upon four principles:

1. The reduction of environmental space.

2. The reduction of unessential visual and auditory environmental stimuli.

3. The establishment of a highly structured daily program.

4. The increase of the stimulus value of the instructional
materials themselves.

Results with 39 pupils after one year (1957-58) indicated the
majority of children in all classes made significantly better rates of
progress in academic areas than they had made previously, with no

15

significant differences between the control and demonstration groups. Subjective evaluation indicated children in the demonstration program made somewhat greater gains in non-academic areas such as social maturity and figure-ground discrimination. The authors made no attempt to isolate contributing factors (indicating direction for future studies) simply stating one or more factors operated to cause a reversal of failure and positive growth.

From an educational point of view, the neurological data and the E.E.G.'s were of least value of any information received; while they might provide diagnostic information they did not provide the descriptive kind of information upon which to plan educational programs. Audiologists and speech pathologists, on the other hand, were found to be very valuable in evaluating and programming for dysfunction in hearing and language areas. Valuable information aims presented on diagnostic procedures, theoretical considerations, and teaching methods.

The study did not indicate the proportion of boys to girls, nor did it clearly indicate the criteria for selection and assignment. Despite these negative criticisms, it is the study most often referred to in considering programs at the elementary school level.

Public School Programs for Emotionally Disturbed Children

Very few controlled research experiments have tested the efficacy of special education for the emotionally disturbed child in the public school. The majority of publications in this area have

been subjective descriptions, prescriptions and clinical case studies.
Contributing to the lack of conclusive evidence has been the frequent
utilization of retrospective studies, questionnaires and historical re-
collections.

Special Classes

Of the different methods used in developing special classes,
the most prevalent today is the structured. The educational techniques
of this method have been adapted and experimentally researched with the
emotionally disturbed by Cruickshank (1961), and Haring and Phillips
(1962).

Cruickshank (1961) presented a lengthy report of his pilot
study with hyperaction children which followed the detailed classroom
methodology and procedures of structured program used with brain-
injured children. Thirty-nine children in two experimental and two
control classes were given pre-and post-tests to show the effects of
special teaching on school achievement, perceptual status and other
factors. Definitive conclusions from the many pages of data and impressions, were not possible because the experiment lacked control of the
variables.

Probably the most valuable research study on methods to date
has been that of Haring and Phillips (1962) working on the hypotheses
that acting-out, aggressive children lacked structure and order in
their environment and emotional life. Results were compared from two
experimental classes of eight children each designed with rigid

17

structure, a control group of fifteen which remained in the regular

class with no specific manipulation by the teacher, and a secondary

control group of fifteen in a loosely structured class framework. The

experimental class showed twice the gain as the control group and

thirty-five times as much gain as the secondary control on measures of

academic achievement. Limitations of the study are the seemingly

brief duration and the limited sampling.

At the present time Hewett (1967) is experimenting with an

engineered, highly structured classroom design based on a behavior

modification theory, being used both in a hospital and four public

schools. His program enlists a hierarchy of educational tasks, re-

wards for learning, teacher structure and an assistant to the teacher.

Hewett refers to his goal through the use of structure as maximizing

the probability of student success leading to replacement of maladap-

tive behavior with adaptive behavior. Results are not available in

any statistical form as yet.

Berkowitz and Rothman (1962) described another methodology

of classroom procedure which, in contrast to the structured approach,

can be termed "permissive". Only one report can be considered research

using a highly permissive self-contained classroom in a public school

setting. Bond (1957) published results of a small class design in

Milwaukee, Wisconsin, consisting of eight boys with normal MA but

severely disturbed. Three returned to regular class by the end of the

year, one was placed in a home, and four remained. Kuenzli (1958) reported on two variables used in a field experiment class at a mental hospital in Minnesota. One variable, male vs female teachers, showed no significant differences. In contrasting the different teaching situations, permissive, moderately structured and highly structured, discipline appeared to be more effective in the high structure but therapy was accomplished more in the permissive phase.

Another interesting program, utilizing both school and community resources, has been organized and described by Donahue and Nichtern (1965). Although no controls or statistics were used, they have reported that over a five-year period out of 31 children served, 21 were returned to their regular classes. This program united the efforts of psychologists, psychiatrists, educators and the volunteer "teacher-mom's" who work in a one-to-one relationship as the child's instructor.

Perhaps the most extensive study in comparing school programs for the Emotionally Handicapped has been done by Eli Bower (1961). In a two year California project, 600 children were selected for placement in special programs designed to provide for and alleviate their emotional and educational deficits while another 600 remained as control groups in their regular classes. In his recommendations, Bower listed the educational procedures that seemed to be the most economical as well as the most effective with emotionally handicapped children. These procedures and approaches were the special class, consultation services for teachers and administrators, provisions for children with learning disabilities and home and hospital educational services for those who cannot attend school. Bower emphasized the importance of early identification and screening for prevention and treatment of incipient emotional problems as the most important aspect of any school special education program.

Other related in-school programs

Several other related in-school programs, aside from the self-contained class, have been described and advocated for use with the emotionally disturbed. The "crisis teacher", who is immediately available in the school to contend with any child's emotional crisis and relieve the regular teacher, as originated by Morse (1962), is a valuable asset to public school programs. The most feasible beginning step in any school is to provide mental health consultation and in-service training for the regular classroom teachers and school administrators in an attempt to positively "modify their perceptions and attitudes of children", the goal of Knoblock and Garcea (1965), and to raise the level of emotional health among the children (Miller, Young, and Morgan, 1963). Bower (1962) stated that such consultation needs to be considered as part of any preventive school program. Newman, Redl, and Kitchener (1964) described use of such a consultant in their "technical assistance" program. Mariner et al. (1961), summarized a two year project of consultation with school personnel, evaluated by means of a test and questionnaire, which took place in San Leandro, California.

Use of individual and group therapy and other clinical services in school settings exists in many programs. Rosen (1961) explained the use of group therapy in two Detroit, Michigan schools as a method of dealing with mental health problems. A multi-disciplinary cooperative approach between school and community resources "to identify and treat as early as possible pre-puberty elementary school children who exhibit a major degree of anti-social and/or a social behavior" is also a Detroit project. However, as Hamil and Scott (1961) stated, the project screens out deeply disturbed children as out of its province and dealt only with children of milder behavioral problems.

In an all-day neighborhood school in New York City, intensive on-the-spot clinical service is maintained for difficult, otherwise un-reachable, children (Rosner, 1957), while in that same city a Junior Guidance Class Program utilized group work, clinical services, recrea-tional programs as well as educational programs (Jay, 1953).

Residential Schools

Related to this review are a few of the residential institu-tions that have applied educational programs in their treatment of emotionally disturbed children. Providing a public school program within a residential setting is offered in Chicago by the Jewish Children's Bureau (Mullen and Blumenthal, 1962), in New York City by Hawthorne Cedar Knolls (Goldsmith et al., 1959), and in Ann Arbor, Michigan by the Children Psychiatric Hospital (Richards, 1963). Talmadge (1963) described a kinesthetic and auditory remedial education approach used in a residential center.

Also of interest is the "Re-Ed" plan of Tennessee and North Carolina, which combined a residential school and camp program for the purpose of providing for disturbed children hoping to return them to their regular schools, as well as training teachers to staff residential schools (Hobbs, 1965). This is a public school, college and community cooperative effort.

Review Summary

In this review of literature various opinions and research on causes of perceptual deficiency and related behavior disorders were presented. Approaches range from specific treatment techniques as typified by the Delacato (1961) method to the general organization of classroom setting and curriculum approach represented by Cruickshank (1961). From these approaches and others have evolved special classrooms for perceptually and/or emotionally handicapped children. It seems, however, that segregation into a separate classroom has occurred mainly from opinion or philosophy rather than research of classroom environments. In relation to emotionally disturbed children there exist few research experiments testing the efficacy of special education for the type child in the public school. The practice of separate classrooms for these children was a consequence of Special Education philosophy of segregation of the mentally retarded child. Approaches other than self-contained classrooms are settings based along the continuum of structured to permissive environment, "crisis" teaching teacher consultation, use of aids, group therapy and itinerant teachings. All these have been attempted with little research justification. There exists a need remaining to discover and justify an approach which is administratively and fiscally possible and one which can treat a significant number of these children within a public school framework.

- - - - - - -

Footnote for this chapter:

1. A report by Sperry (1964) suggest current studies of the brain may help resolve some of the differences among various theories of brain functioning as they have developed in the past. Before-and-after tests, longitudinal studies, etc., on animals and on humans who have had neuro-surgery indicates the transfer of learning (visual, motor, etc.) and memory from one hemisphere to the other occurs readily under normal conditions, establishing a duplicate set of traces, either at the time of learning or later on demand. Man tends to use this second method and certain kinds of damage prevent or distort the trans-mittal of information from the storage area to the requesting side (usually the dominant side). This is especially true in language functions and it can be seen how difficulties can arise when the stor-age area is not in the ordering side.

STATEMENT OF PROBLEM AND PROCEDURE

Problem

At present not all the services for emotionally and perceptually handicapped children combined do more than a small part of the
total job required (Axline, 1947; Beilin, 1950; Bettelheim, 1949;
D'Evelyn, 1957; Devereau, 1956; Freud, 1928, 1937; Hirshberg, 1953;
Jacobson and Eaegre, 1959; Lippman, 1956; Medley and Mitzel, 1959;
Moustakas, 1953, 1956; Mass, 1959; Neill, 1960; Newman, 1956; Pearson,
1938, 1949, 1954, 1957; Redl and Wattenberg, 1951; Redl and Wineman,
1951, 1952; Rogers, 1942, 1951; Slavson, 1954; Strauss and Lehtinen,
1947). There is a growing realization that existing services leave
much to be desired, and the great neglect heretofore of the emotionally
and perceptually handicapped child's educational needs is becoming more
clearly perceived (Beilin, 1959; Cruickshank, Bentzen, Ratzeberg, and
Tannhauser, 1961; Galanter, 1959; Haring, Sterm, and Cruickshank, 1958;
Hay, 1953; Hayden, 1956; Heil, Powell, and Feifer, 1960; Hymes, 1949,
1955; Jacobson and Faegre, 1959; Nass, 1959, Phillips, 1956, 1957a,
1957b, 1957c, 1957d, 1958a, 1958b, 1959, 1960; Phillips and Haring,
1959; Phillips and Johnston, 1954; Phillips, Wiener, and Haring, 1960;
Prescott, 1938, 1957; Strauss and Lehtinen, 1947).

It is uncommon to find a both educationally and emotionally
constructive environment for the emotionally and perceptually handicapped child; very few plans for operating such programs exist in the

24

public schools, and those in private settings are very expensive (Bettelheim, 1949; Freud, 1928, 1937; Newman, 1956; Pearson, 1949, 1954; Redl and Wattenberg, 1951; Redl and Wineman, 1951, 1952; Reid and Gagan, 1952; Slavson, 1954). Few or no models of how such a program could be carried on are available for study, and there exist few programs for training teachers to cope with problems of the emotionally disturbed child (Phillips, 1957d).

Confronted with the task of the re-education and re-adaptation of emotionally and perceptually handicapped children, the following questions need to be focused on in the public school programs:

1. What kind of atmosphere and school structure would best serve to undo pathological behavior and serve the goal of rehabilitation?

2. What combination of children should be grouped together into classes?

3. What type of public school settings for emotionally and perceptually handicapped children is administratively and financially possible yet meet the criteria of helping the majority of emotionally and perceptually disturbed children?

Tempered by the very real situation of designing a program which can be funded by a public school system and yet meet the needs of all children requiring specialized assistance, the problem becomes not that of setting up a "showcase" program involving 10-15 children, but of developing a program that can involve the majority of these

25

children.

Poudre R-1 School District would hope to have sufficient funds to support a program for emotionally and perceptually handicapped children when the Title III Funding is discontinued, possibly in August of 1968. The purpose of this study was to gain evidence toward answering question 1 listed above.

Procedure

A comparative study of classroom setting for emotionally and perceptually handicapped children was made in the Poudre School District, Fort Collins, Colorado. This study was of the effects of different classroom placement on these children.

Selection of Subjects

From 60 children diagnosed as perceptually or emotionally handicapped, 18 children were selected randomly. These children were defined under the following three categories:

1. Mild emotional dysfunction with mild organicity.

2. More intensive emotional dysfunction with mild organicity.

3. Functional emotional problems with organicity secondary or non-existent.

These children were identified by the following procedures: (1) psychological evaluation to include academic achievement tests; (2) neurological examination if desired; (3) speech and hearing evaluation; (4) pediatric examination; (5) social worker evaluation of en-

26

vironmental factors; (6) teacher evaluation; and (7) staffing of the child by combined Mental Health Center and Larimer Children's Center Staff. Criterion for selection also includes an age requirement of 6 to 12 years of age.

The subjects were then assigned at random to one of the following groups:

1. Comparison Group.--This group received no designed manipulation of classroom setting or teacher. They attended school all day in different regular classrooms.

2. Educo-Therapy Group.--This group attended a regular school classroom for one-half the school day and the Educo-Therapy classroom for the second half. This Educo-Therapy classroom had a teacher ratio of one to six children and both the classroom and curriculum were designed specifically to assist the emotionally and perceptually handicapped child.

3. Heterogeneous Group.--These six children were placed in a regular classroom setting with eighteen other regular students. A second teacher qualified in the areas of emotionally disturbed children was added to the classroom to work specifically with the six emotionally and perceptually handicapped students. These children attended this classroom the full day.

The groups were similar in that all had been diagnosed as emotionally and/or perceptually handicapped and they all attended a full day of school. The differences were in the extent of treatment given, the nature of the treatment given, and the setting it was given in. The comparison group child had no designed treatment program and followed a regular classroom procedure. The Educo-Therapy child attended regular school one-half a school day where he followed the regular procedures of his class. The second half of his day he attended the Educo-Therapy Center where he and five other children were given remedial academic instruction, psychomotor training, and individual and group therapy. The academic and psychomotor work was done by a specialist teacher with the therapy mainly handled by a psychologist or social worker. The heterogeneous child attended a regular class all day. This class was composed of 18 regular children and 6 children diagnosed as emotionally and/or perceptually handicapped. The class had a regular teacher and a second teacher whose main responsibility was to assist the six children. These children as did the Educo-Therapy children also received remedial academic instruction, psychomotor training and individual and group therapy. They were, however, seated randomly in the class and were encouraged and assisted in taking part in those class activities which they were capable of. Emphasis was placed on those class activities which allowed integration and group involvement for the six children with the other eighteen regular children.

The intent of this research was to discover which of these classroom settings or environments was most effective in creating a more positive self-concept and higher academic efficiency. The following hypotheses were tested:

1. There will be significant differences in academic gains between the three groups.

2. There will be significant differences in self-concept gains between the three groups.

A significance level of .05 was used for rejecting or accepting the hypotheses.

Description of the Subjects

Table 1 shows the distribution of the three groups of children on grade, age and sex variables.

Table 1. Distribution of the three groups of children on grade, age and sex.

	Grade			Age			Sex		
	H.	E.T.	C.	H.	E.T.	C.	H.	E.T.	C.
1	3	3	3	8.2	8-11	8-3	F	F	F
2	3	3	3	8.2	8-7	8-4	M	M	M
3	3	2	3	9.3	7-1	8-1	M	M	M
4	2	2	4	7-10	8-6	9-11	M	M	M
5	2	3	3	7-11	9-1	9-3	M	M	M
6	3	3	2	8-1	8-3	8-0	M	M	M

Summary

				Mean Age					
4	3rd	4-3rd	1-4th	8-3	8-5	8-6	5M	5M	5M
2	2nd	2-2nd	4-3-d 1-2nd				1F	1F	1F

Although randomly selected, each group had one third grade girl in it and each group had one boy nine years old who had been retained in the

29

third grade. Each group also had one child in the second grade who had received positive evidence on an E.E.G. of brain damage. The closeness of other variables in the grouping also is reflected in the Mean Full Scale IQ Score of each of the groups. These mean scores are within two and two-tenths IQ points of each other (96.1 to 98.3).

Each child reflected markedly different social histories, and personality constellations. Frequently the problems of the child appeared to be a by-product of the natural order or disorder of the family. Almost all the families which bred and nurtured these children demonstrated readily identifiable, but not easily alterable, social pathology. Some of these families functioned as if their integrity depended upon the preservation of the very pathology identifiable as contributing to the disorganization of their child.

Despite individual differences and specific problems, all the children were distractible, impulse driven, and motivated primarily by internal stimuli frequently unrelated to their external environment. Disabilities extended into nearly every area of motor and perceptual organization. Their performance was unpatterned and unpredictable. This variability was extensively reflected in all psychological and educational testing. Intra- and inter-test variability was the rule.

Description of the Classroom

The children in the comparison group were in regular sized classrooms with 25 to 30 other student. None of the children were in the same school.

The children in the Educo-Therapy Group attended class in a converted quonset. Individual booths were assigned each child and most of his school work was done in his individual booth. Adjacent to the classroom was the play therapy and group therapy rooms. The playground of the regular school next to the quonsets was used for physical activity. The location of the Educo-Therapy Center was from 6 to 10 miles from the child's regular school and required transportation for the child to and from the school each day.

The children in the Heterogeneous Group attended school at a regular school in the center of the school district. The classroom was a converted kingergarten classroom, larger than the usual classroom size.

Classroom Treatment and Curriculum Processes of the
Educo-Therapy Center and Heterogeneous Group

The treatment and curriculum processes are centered around the following three areas:

1. Academic--Individual remedial instruction was given each child in the academic area in which he is substandard.

2. Expressive--Remediation of the communication methods of the child, either verbal or non-verbal in nature, was worked on. Individual or group therapy was the main treatment process with efforts made to preserve the child's "uniqueness" but also to modify those aspects of

31

expression which indicated faulty interpretation and exploration of his environment.

3. Physical or Psychomotor--Regardless of an emotional or neurological diagnosis as a child's main difficulty, most of the children showed common difficulties in "body image". Balance, agility, rhythm, and coordination were some of the areas that a child may have been having difficulty. Sensory motor training was given to the child in those areas he was deficient. Balancing boards, eye movement (tracking) exercises, eye-hand coordination exercises, jumping, skipping, throwing were only a few of the methods used in helping the child gain skill in coordination and which allowed the child to review and re-examine the actions of his body parts and the combinations that were possible for more effective performance.

No fine differentiations were made as to categorizing where each of the areas were being treated. For example, good therapeutic gains in the expressive area were often made by the teacher as she was assisting the child with the academic problems. The psychologist or social worker found many occasions in play therapy where academic and physical skills were assisted.

Daily diaries were kept on each child in both the Educo-Therapy and the Heterogeneous setting. Both gains and difficulties were noted in each of the three mentioned treatment areas. Step by step remediation was decided upon and followed.

The Educo-Therapy Center social worker or psychologist

worked with the Educo-Therapy and Heterogeneous classroom children on a scheduled basis and at other times on the request of the teacher.

Parent Counseling

If a parent desired individual assistance, weekly conferences with the psychologist or social worker were scheduled.

Parent group therapy for parents of the Educo-Therapy and Heterogeneous children was held every other week at the Educo-Therapy Center. The meetings were held in the evening allowing both parents to attend. The psychologist, social worker, and teacher of the children whose parents were in a particular group attended all meetings. The initial meetings were structured. The general behavioral and academic problems of children were explained and reasons given for some of the difficulties. Each parent was encouraged to describe his child and his method of handling the child and if possible to indicate why he feels the child is having difficulty. After the initial unfamiliarity was lessened, the groups were guided into interaction with one another where their own behaviors and perceptions of the world and one another became the central focus.

Description of the Data

Data was collected at the start of the school year and at its close. All children were in the second, third, or fourth grade and were given at the school's beginning a Wechsler Intelligence Scale for Children, a Bender Gestalt Test, the Wide Range Achievement Test and

the Science Research Association Achievement Test. In addition, "A
Picture Game", "A Class Play", and "Thinking About Yourself" portions
of Bower and Lambert's "Process for In-School Screening of Children with
Emotional Handicaps" were given to each child. The children received
the same battery with alternate forms used when possible at the end of
the school year.

Description of Evaluation Materials

Science Research Associates Achievement
Series Form C-D (Louis P. Thorpe, D.)
Welty Lefever, Robert A. Naslund

The SRA Achievement Series is a comprehensive test battery
that measures what students have learned as their ability to apply that
knowledge.

The Achievement Series consists of five batteries, including
two primary batteries scored by the teacher with stencils, two machine-
scorable batteries for grades 1-2 and 3-4; and a multi-level battery
for grades 4-9, designed for machine or hand scoring.

The two Achievement Series batteries used were:

Grades 1-2. Designed to be used in the first grade and through-
out the second grade, this battery consists of reading and arithmetic
tests which come in separate booklets. Students write their answers
directly in the booklets. Stencils are available for scoring.

Grades 2-4. Appropriate for students from the end of the second grade through the beginning of the fourth grade, this battery

measures achievement in reading, arithmetic, and language arts. It may be purchased in a single book which includes all three tests, or in three separate booklets. Answer sheets are not necessary as responses are written in the test booklets. Stencils can be used for scoring.

Wechsler Intelligence Scale for Children
(David Wechsler)

The WISC consists of twelve tests which, like the adult scales, are divided into two subgroups identified as Verbal and Performance. Most of the verbal tests correlate better with each other than with tests of the performance group, and vice versa. But, while the tests identified as verbal and performance differ as these labels indicate, they each tap other factors, among them non-intellective ones, which cut across the groups to produce other classifications or categories that are equally important to consider in evaluating the individual's performance.

The tests of the Scale are grouped as follows--Verbal: Information, Comprehension, Arithmetic, Similarities, Vocabulary, Digit Span; Performances: Picture Completion, Picture Arrangement, Block Design, Object Assembly, Coding, Mazes. Both Verbal and Performance IQ's as well as a Full Scale I.Q. are obtainable with this test.

Wide Range Achievement Test
(J.F. Jastak and S.F. Jastak)

The Wide Range Achievement Test (hereafter called WRAT) was first standardized in 1936 as a convenient tool for the study of the basic school subjects of reading (word recognition and pronunciation).

written spelling, and arithmetic computation. It was designed as an adjunct to tests of intelligence and behavior adjustment.

Bender Gestalt (Lauretta Bender)

The Bender-Gestalt test consists of nine simple designs, each of which is presented to a subject for him to copy on a sheet of paper. These designs, along with several others, were originally used by Wertheimer in his studies of visual perception. Dr. Lauretta Bender selected from Wertheimer's nine designs and incorporated these into a test for clinical use. The results of her studies with the nine designs are presented by her in a monograph, A Visual Motor Gestalt Test and Its Clinical Use, published in 1938. Since the publication of her monograph, Bender's test has come into widespread use as a clinical instrument. It has been used to estimate maturation, intelligence, psychological disturbances, and the effects of injury to the cortex, and to follow the effects of convulsive therapy.

Process for In-School Screening of Children
With Emotional Handicaps (Nadine M. Lambert and Eli M. Bower)

As of the time of the publication of this paper, there are seven instruments in the screening process intended for general research use: Three were used in this study and are explained in detail.

1. Behavior Rating of Pupils (all grades)

2. Class Pictures (primary grades)

3. A Class Play (elementary grades)

   (Section II) elicits from each pupil an indication of

the roles he would prefer, or which he thinks other people would select for him. This section has thirty different quartets of the twenty roles, with a question aimed at finding out how the child sees himself in relation to each role.

4. Student Survey (secondary grades)

5. A Picture Game (primary grades)

Description: A Picture Game is designed to give a measure of young children's perception of self.

A Picture Game consists of 66 pictures, including two sample pictures. Each picture is illustrative of normal home and school relationships and events. With the exception of the two sample cards and the first ten pictures, each picture is emotionally neutral in the portrayal of the relationship or event. The child is asked to sort each picture into one of two categories: "This is a happy picture" or "This is a sad picture". The sorting is done by placing each picture in the "happy" or "sad" side of a two-compartment box which has a happy face shown on one compartment and a sad face on the other. The child categorizes each picture in accordance with his perception of it.

6. Thinking About Yourself (elementary grades)

Description: The purpose of Thinking About Yourself is to elicit from the pupil himself an intra-self measure of the relationship between a pupil's perception of his environment and his conception of what it ought to be. What is looked for is the degree of discrepancy between a pupil's self-perception and an ideal self, between his perception of himself as he _is_ and as he would like to be.

Many pupils with serious emotional problems cannot bring themselves to disclose their difficulties in writing, or are uncomfortable about disclosing them. Their responses will therefore very much resemble those of other children in the class. These youngsters are most likely to be screened by teachers and peers.

There are other pupils, however, who do not manifest their difficulties to teachers or peers, but who rise to the opportunity to express inner discomfort and _can_ communicate their disturbance on a self rating instrument. Since the average discrepancy between self and _ideal_ self has been found to discriminate between pupils with emotional problems and those with normal behavior adjustment, Thinking About Yourself provides a meaningful and useful screening dimension not available from teacher or peer ratings.

7. A Self Test (secondary grades).

FINDINGS OF THE STUDY

The present study was undertaken to test the effectiveness of three different public school settings for emotionally and perceptually handicapped children. These settings consisted of (1) regular school placement of the emotionally and perceptually handicapped child with no designed manipulation of his class environment, (2) a half day placement in a regular class and half in a class framework designed for remediation of the students' particular difficulties, and (3) a full day setting where six emotionally and perceptually handicapped children were placed in a classroom with eighteen regular children. A second teacher was added to deal primarily with these children.

In presenting the findings the hypotheses have been presented in order. Statistical techniques utilized in reporting the data include the nonparametric Mann-Whitney U-test for gain comparison of the three groups with each other and the Randomization Test for Matched Pairs for comparison of within group pre-post test scores. Because of the varied opinions concerning what the Bender Gestalt Test measures, the data concerning the Bender Gestalt will be treated separately after the academic change and self-concept change data is treated.

Analysis of Specific Hypotheses

Hypothesis 1

"There will be significant difference in academic gains between the three groups." Tables 2a, 2b, 3, and 4 contain a comparison of the three groups on WISC, SRA, and WRAT gains. From Tables 2a, 2b, 3, and 4 it may be seen that there were significant differences in the three groups.

Table 2a. WISC raw score means

	Comparison		Educo-Therapy		Heterogeneous	
	Pre	Post	Pre	Post	Pre	Post
Information	9.5	9.5	8.6	9.8	10.0	10.66
SD	1.38	2.12	2.36	2.26	2.88	4.12
Comprehension	9.8	8.3	8.8	6.0	7.67	8.67
SD	2.47	3.33	2.36	.81	3.03	2.55
Arithmetic	5.6	7.0	6	6.5	5.50	7.0
SD	1.28	1.15	.81	1.20	2.14	2.83
S.M.	6.0	8.3	6.0	10.0	5.83	8.33
SD	2.0	2.10	1.21	1.04	1.96	2.83
Vocab.	25.5	26.16	24.16	29.16	23.0	24.17
SD	4.39	3.39	5.63	3.81	6.83	8.92
D.S.	7.16	7.83	7.16	7.5	6.5	7.3
SD	.75	.72	1.11	.50	1.89	1.93
P.C.	11	12.17	10	12.16	9.5	9.83
SD	2.44	2.23	2.08	2.15	2.06	2.13
P.A.	19	31.5	19.33	29.00	19.3	25.83
SD	6.72	9.18	9.22	7.39	6.96	6.97
B.D.	10.83	19.8	8.50	14.50	11.33	13.67
SD	7.16	6.66	3.35	4.18	7.39	8.89
O.A.	20.6	21.5	17.67	19.67	15.5	20.0
SD	2.17	3.34	2.50	2.24	4.36	4.69
Coding	23.8	29.16	23.50	28.33	21.8	20.5
SD	4.52	7.06	10.56	5.24	6.60	8.97

Table 2b. WISC Subtest data, Comparison vs. Heterogeneous vs. Educo-
Therapy[a]

	Comparison vs. Heterogeneous		Comparison vs. Educo-Therapy		Heterogeneous vs. Educo-Therapy	
	U	P	U	P	U	P
Info.	13	.242 N.S.	17	.469 N.S.	14	.294 N.S.
Comp.	18	.531 N.S.	11	.155 N.S.	9	.090 N.S.
Arith.	11	.155 N.S.	18	.531 N.S.	13	.242 N.S.
Sim.	10	.120 N.S.	17	.469 N.S.	10	.120 N.S.
Vocab.	10	.120 N.S.	11	.155 N.S.	17	.469 N.S.
D.S.	15	.350 N.S.	15	.350 N.S.	11	.155 N.S.
P.C.	12	.197 N.S.	8	.066 N.S.	9	.090 N.S.
P.A.	9	.090 N.S.	10	.120 N.S.	18	.531 N.S.
B.D.	1	.002 Sig. (Favors Comparison)	5	.021 Sig. (Favors Comparison)	8	.066 N.S.
O.A.	12	.197 N.S.	8	.066 N.S.	13	.242 N.S.
Coding	16	.409 N.S.	5	.021 Sig (Favors Comparison)	7	.047 Sig.(Favors Educo-Therapy)

[a]Statistical Treatment: Mann Whitney U

41

Table 3. SRA scores, Comparison, vs. Educo-Therapy vs. Heterogeneous

	Comparison vs. Heterogeneous		Comparison vs. Educo-Therapy		Educo-Therapy vs. Heterogeneous	
	U	P	U	P	U	P
Compre-hension	5	.021 Sig. (Favors Hetero.)	9	.090 N.S.	14	.294 N.S.
Vocabulary	14	.294 N.S.	14	.294 N.S.	17	.469 N.S.
Total Read-ing	11	.155 N.S.	7	.047 Sig. (Favors Educo.)	14	.294 N.S.
Cap & Punc.	9	.452 N.S.	2	.071 N.S.	3	.200 N.S.
Gram Usage	8	.365 N.S.	7	.500 N.S.	5	.429 N.S.
Spelling	1	.016 Sig. (Favors Hetero.)	4	.196 N.S.	4	.314 N.S.
Total Lang Arts	8	.365 N.S.	3	.125 N.S.	2	.114 N.S.
Concepts	9	.452 N.S.	5	.021 Sig. (Favors Educo.)	14	.294 N.S.
Reasoning	16	.409 N.S.	10	.120 N.S.	16	.409 N.S.
Computation	3	.008 Sig. (Favors Hetero.)	11	.155 N.S.	10	.120 N.S.
Total Arith	6	.032 Sig. (Favors Hetero.)	6	.032 Sig. (Favors Educo.)	17	.469 N.S.
Composite	7	.047 Sig. (Favors Hetero.)	8	.066 N.S.	17	.469 N.S.

Table 4. WRAT scores, Comparison vs. Educo-Therapy vs. Heterogeneous

	Comparison vs. Heterogeneous		Comparison vs. Educo-Therapy		Educo-Therapy vs. Heterogeneous	
	U	P	U	P	U	P
Reading	9	.090 N.S.	9	.090 N.S.	4	.013 Sig. (Favors Educo-Therapy)
Spelling	10	.120 N.S.	0	.001 Sig. (Favors Educo-Therapy)	12	.197 N.S.
Arith.	16	.409 N.S.	17	.469 N.S.	16	.409 N.S.

There were fourteen areas of significant difference between the scores of the three groups. Nine of these were in favor of either the Heterogeneous or Educo-Therapy Group as compared to the Comparison Group. Two favored the Educo-Therapy Group as compared to the Heterogeneous Group, and three favored the Comparison Group as compared to the Heterogeneous Group or Educo-Therapy Group. On the basis of these findings hypothesis 1 was accepted.

Hypothesis 2

"There will be significant difference in self-concept gains between the three groups." Table 5 contains a comparison of the three groups on self-concept scores.

From Table 5 it can be seen that there were significant dif-

43

ferences in the three groups. Five significant differences existed be-
tween the groups. Four of these favor the Heterogeneous and Educo-
Therapy Group over the Comparison Group. One favors the Heterogeneous
Group over the Educo-Therapy Group. On the basis of these findings
Hypothesis 2 was accepted.

Analysis of Bender Gestalt Scores

The writer prefers to regard the Bender Gestalt as both a
test of visual-motor perception and as a test of emotional adjustment
and personality. Table 6 indicates that there are significant differences in one of the three groups.

Showing the significant difference between the Educo-Therapy
Group and the Heterogeneous in favor of the Educo-Therapy Group the
acceptance of Hypothesis 2 is further supported by this data.

Table 5. Process for in-school screening of children with emotional
handicaps.[a]

	Comparison vs. Heterogeneous		Comparison vs. Educo-Therapy		Heterogeneous vs. Educo-Therapy	
	U	P	U	P	U	P
Picture Game	17	.469 N.S.	6	.032 Sig. (Favors Educo-Therapy)	7	.047 Sig. (Favors Hetero.)
Thinking About Self	0	.001 Sig. (Favors Hetero.)	3	.008 Sig. (Favors Educo-Therapy)	12	.197 N.S.
Class Play	4	.013 Sig. (Favors Hetero.)	12	.197 N.S.	10	.120 N.S.

Table 6. Bender Gestalt Scores[a]

Gains of	n_1	n_2	U	P (Two tailed)
Educo vs. Heterogeneous	6	6	4	.025 sig.
Heterogeneous vs. Comparison	6	6	14	.588 N.S.
Educo vs. Comparison	6	6	14	.588 N.S.

[a]Statistical Treatment: Mann Whitney U. (Test of the significance of difference between two independent samples.)

Summary

The findings related to each of the two major hypotheses were presented in this chapter. Additional data concerning within group changes are presented in a discussion of the findings which follows.

DISCUSSION

Included in this chapter are a discussion of the overall results of the study, a discussion of each hypothesis and a discussion
of other relevant data collected during the study.

Overall Results

Overall, the results of this study suggested that planned and
specialized methods and settings for children with educational and perceptual difficulties can contribute significantly to the remediation of
these difficulties. A comparison (Tables 9 through 20), however, of
pre- and post-test gains showed all groups, including the Comparison
Group, made significant academic gains. Critical to this was the data
of Tables 18 and 19 which showed that the self-concepts of the Educo-
Therapy and Heterogeneous Groups were more favorable, but the self-concepts of the Comparison Group were significantly more negative.

Discussion of the Hypotheses

Hypothesis 1

"There will be significant difference in academic gains between the three groups."

Eleven scores were obtained on the WISC data (Tables 2a, 2b).
The Comparison Group made significant improvement on Block Design over
the Heterogeneous Group and approached significance (.066) in the area
of Object Assembly. The Comparison Group made significant improvement
on Block Design and Coding over the Educo-Therapy Group. The Educo-

46

Therapy Group made significant gains on Coding over the Heterogeneous Group and approached significance (.066) in the area of Block Design. It was difficult for the writer to explain the significant difference in favor of the Comparison over Heterogeneous on Block Design and over the Educo-Therapy in Block Design and Coding. Increased ability in Visual Motor Coordination, Perceptual Organization and Psychomotor Speed with the related high motivation, persistence and attention would appear to relate closely with increased mental alertness and academic performance. However, other academic and achievement scores do not bear out this same significant change in reference to the other groups.

One should keep in mind that the reliability of the individual subtest scores on the WISC is low. Judgement with respect to the WISC subtest differences should be made with caution. More weight has been placed by the writer on the changes made on the other tests than the changes in subtest WISC scores.

On the WRAT scores (Tables 4, 9, 10, 11) significant differences were gained by the Educo-Therapy Group over the Comparison Group in the area of Spelling and by the Educo-Therapy Group over the Heterogeneous Group in the area of Reading. This may point out that the practice of integrating the Heterogeneous children into the regular reading group at the level they are reading is not as effective as the individualized reading done with the Educo-Therapy children.

The SRA scores (Tables 3, 12, 13, 14) gained by the Educo-Therapy Group and the Heterogeneous Group are significantly higher than those of the Comparison Group. Increase in mean composite score when stated in terms of grade equivalency growth is from second grade-five months to third grade-one month for the Comparison Group, third grade-one month to fourth grade-three months for the Educo-Therapy Group and second grade-eight months to fourth grade-three months for the Heterogeneous Group. This represents achievement growth over an eight month period of time as measured on alternate forms of the SRA Achievement Test.

Hypothesis 2

"There will be significant differences in self-concept gains between the three groups."

Tables 5, 18, and 19 indicate that there are significant differences. The Comparison Group post-test scores were significantly different than their pre-test scores toward the direction of increasing negative self-concept. The Heterogeneous Group made significant pre-post-test changes toward the direction of a more positive self-concept. In relationship to each other both the Educo-Therapy Group and Heterogeneous Group changed significantly when compared to the Comparison Group. All changes were in the direction of a more positive self-concept. The Heterogeneous Group was significantly different than the Educo-Therapy Group on the Picture Game section. This indicates that the child is seeing his environment as more accepting of his and that situations have a more happy context. The Heterogeneous classroom where the child is mixed with the regular children gives the child the

48

opportunity of gaining acceptance under controlled conditions. The child is able to perceive and interact with more healthy children as contrasted to the Educo-Therapy setting where each of the six children are interacting with each other.

Discussion of the Bender Gestalt Test Data

As can be seen from Tables 6, 20, and 21 there does exist a significant difference between Educo-Therapy scores and Heterogeneous scores in favor of Educo-Therapy.

In looking at the scores it can be seen that the children who changed most were those who were highly deviate in their Bender Gestalt patterns. There were more highly deviate scores in the Educo-Therapy Group than the Heterogeneous Group. The change then on the Bender although appearing as a significant difference favoring the Educo-Therapy setting over the Heterogeneous one must be tempered by the fact that the weights of a unit change toward a normal Bender are not equal. The writer was interested in the question of whether there existed an agreement or correlation in the size of change among the four test batterys given. Mean scores changes were plotted in three factor areas: (1) Verbal Comprehension, (2) Arithmetic, and (3) Perceptual Organization. Table 7 portrays the degree of relationship of test score change in these areas among the four test batterys. As can be seen from the Table, the group (E.T.) who had the highest amount of change on the WISC in the Verbal Comprehension area also had the highest amount of change

49

on the WRAT and SRA Achievement Test in this area. No other significant consistency can be noted between the four test batterys as they apply to the three factors.

Of interest to the writer also was the scores of the pre- and post-test WISC. Table 8 summarizes the WISC findings. In comparing the three groups the Comparison Group made significant gains on the Performance Scale and Full Scale IQ Scores. The Heterogeneous Group made significant gains on the Full Scale Score and the Educo-Therapy Group made significant gains on the Performance Scale.

Table 7. Mean score change three factor areas

	Verbal Comprehension			Arithmetical			Perceptual Organization		
	H.	E.T.	C.	H.	E.T.	C.	H.	E.T.	C.

WISC Scores: I.Q. norms nearest tenth of a point

	Verbal Comprehension			Arithmetical			Perceptual Organization		
	H.	E.T.	C.	H.	E.T.	C.	H.	E.T.	C.
Information	1.01↓	0.2↑	0.3↑						
Comprehension	No Change↓	2.6↓	1.3↓						
Arithmetical				1.1↑	0.5↓	1.3↑			
Similarities	1.0↑	3.3↑	1.3↑						
Vocabulary	0.5↓	0.9↑	1.3↓						
D.S.									
P.C.							0.2↓	1.4↑	0.3↑
P.A.							1.0↑	1.0↑	0.8↑
B.D.							No Change	1.5↑	1.3↑
O.A.							1.0↑	No Change	0.3↓
C.									

WRAT Scores: Raw Score Changes

	Verbal Comprehension			Arithmetical			Perceptual Organization		
Reading	4↑	9↑	6↑						
Spelling	7↑	10↑	5↑						
Arithmetical				5↑	5↑	4.5↑			

SRA Scores: Raw Score Changes

	Verbal Comprehension			Arithmetical			Perceptual Organization		
Comprehension	5↑	8↑	3						
Vocabulary	8↑	6↑	5↑						
Arithmetical Concepts				8↑	10↑	6↑			
Arithmetical Reasoning				8↑	7↑	4↑			
Computation				4↑	9↑	1↑			

Bender Gestalt

	Verbal Comprehension			Arithmetical			Perceptual Organization		
Raw Score changes							19↑	25↑	22↑

Table 8. WISC scores, Pre-post test IQ change

	V.S.		P.S.		F.S.	
	Pre	Post	Pre	Post	Pre	Post
Comparison						
Mean	93.2	93.2	104.5	114.6	98.3	103.5
SD	7.3	8.8	2.8	2.3	1.9	1.9
E.T.						
Mean	93.3	93.8	99.5	105.5	96.2	99.5
S.D.	7.3	5.7	10.9	2.5	2.8	2.4
Hetero						
Mean	93.6	96.7	100.2	102.8	96.3	98.0
SD	17.2	15.7	13.3	15.2	16.5	16.8

SUMMARY, CONCLUSION, AND RECOMMENDATIONS

Summary

Need for the Study

Increased attention is being given to planning for the education of children with characteristics placing them far enough from the norm to be labeled "atypical". A large group of these children are labeled emotionally handicapped or perceptually handicapped. Few public school settings exist for these children and those are expensive. It is important that public school classroom settings which are not financially prohibitive be explored and those settings which allow remediation of the majority of these children in a public school framework be advanced as possible approaches for assisting these children.

Purpose of the Study

The purpose of this study was to see which of two classroom settings was of most value in remediating the deviate academic and behavioral style of elementary school children labeled as emotionally and perceptually handicapped.

Methods and Procedures

This study included eighteen children selected randomly from sixty children who were divided into three groups as follows:

Comparison Group.--This group received no designed manipulation of classroom setting curriculum or teacher.

Educo-Therapy Group.--This group attended the regular school classroom for one-half the school day and the Educo-Therapy classroom for the second half. The classroom had a teacher ratio of one to six children and both the classroom and curriculum were designed specifically to assist the emotionally and perceptually handicapped child.

Heterogeneous Group.--These six children were placed in a regular classroom setting with eighteen other regular students. A second teacher qualified in the area of emotionally disturbed children was added to the classroom to work specifically with the six emotionally and perceptually handicapped students.

The criteria deemed most appropriate for this study was academic improvement and positive self-concept change. Comparisons, using appropriate statistical techniques were made between the groups at the start of the school year and at the end.

Conclusion

The general conclusion of this investigation was as follows:

Children in the two experimental groups did attain significantly higher and more positive academic and self-concept changes than those in the Comparison Group. This indicates that specialized settings and methods are significantly helpful in remediating the emotionally and perceptually handicapped child.

Recommendations

1. The small number of children in the research design is a statistical handicap. One non-producing child, as is typified by one in

54

the Heterogeneous Group, can seriously limit the mean change of the group. Larger numbers should be used.

    2. Different measures of behavioral change and self-concept change should be explored and some added to this type of study. Teacher ratings may be helpful.

REFERENCES

Axline, Virginia. 1947. Play Therapy. Houghton Mifflin, Boston, Mass.

Balow, B. 1966. The Emotionally and Socially Handicapped. Review of Educational Research, Education of Exceptional Children, American Educational Research Association. 36:120 133. February.

Beilin, Harry. 1959. "Teachers' and Children's Attitudes Toward the Behavioral Problems of Children: A Reappraisal." Child Development. 30:9 25.

Bend, E. A. 1957. "Consider the Emotionally Disturbed Child," Nation's Schools, 60:35-39, August.

Berkowitz, P. A. and E. P. Rothman. 1962. The Disturbed Child. New York University Press, New York.

Bettelheim, Bruno. 1949. Love is Not Enough. Free Press, New York.

Bower, E. M. 1961. The Education of Emotionally Handicapped Children. California State Department of Education, Sacramento, California.

Bower, E. M. 1962. Comparison of the Characteristics of Identified Emotionally Disturbed Children with Other Children in Classes. In E. Philip Trapp and Philip Himelstein (Eds.). Readings on the Exceptional Child. Appleton-Century-Crofts, New York.

Broca. 1861. Reported by J. Dejerine. Memories de la Societe de Biologie, Paris, p. 81. (Original not seen; cited by Donald Mahler. 1964. Instructional Planning for Educationally Handicapped Children. Orinda Union School District, Orinda, California.)

Cruickshank, William M., Frances A. Bentzen, Frederick H. Ratzenburg, and Marion T. Tannhauser. 1961. Teaching Methodology for Brain Injured and Hyperactive Children. Syracuse University Press, Syracuse, New York.

Delacato, Carl H. 1961. The treatment and Prevention of Reading Disorders. Charles C. Thomas, Springfield, Illinois.

D'Evelyn, Katherine. 1957. Meeting Children's Emotional Needs. Prentice-Hall, Englewood Cliffs, New Jersey.

Devereaux, George. 1956. Therapeutic Education. Harper, New York.

Donahue, G. T. and S. Nichtern. 1965. Teaching the Troubled Child. The Free Press, New York.

Eisenson, John. 1958. "Aphasia and Dyslexia in Children," Bulletin from the Orton Society. 8:3.

Freud, Anna. 1928. Introduction to the Technique of Child Analysis. Nervous and Mental Diseases Publishing, Washington.

Freud, Anna. 1937. The Ego and the Mechanisms of Defense. Hogarth, London.

Freud, Sigmund. 1891. On Aphasia. International University Press, Inc., New York.

Freud, Sigmund. 1954. The Origins of Psychoanalysis. Basic Books, New York.

Galanter, Eugene. 1959. Automatic Teaching: The State of the Art. John Wiley and Sons, New York.

Gates, Arthur. 1947. The Improvement of Reading. The Macmillan Co., New York.

Goldsmith, J. H., Krohn, R. Ochroch, and N. Kaga. 1959. "Changing the Delinquents' Concept of School." American Journal of Ortho-psychiatry. 29:249-265.

Hamil, B. M., and H. M. Stitt. 1962. "Detroit School-Community Behavior Projects." Journal of Michigan Medical Society. 61:1119-1123. September.

Haring, Norris F., George Stern, and William M. Cruickshank. 1958. Attitudes of Educators Toward Exceptional Children. Syracuse University Press, Syracuse, New York.

Haring, N. G., and E. L. Phillips. 1962. Educating Emotionally Dis-turbed Children. McGraw-Hill Book Co., New York.

Hay, L. 1953. "A New School Channel for Helping the Troubled Child." American Journal of Orthopsychiatry. 23:676-690.

Hayden, E. J. 1956. "The Education of Detroit's Socially Maladjusted Children," Action. 9:5-7.

Head, Henry. 1915. Hughlings Jackson on Aphasis and Kindred Affection of Speech. Hutner, New York, p. 89.

Heil, Louis W., Marion Powell, and Irwin Feifer. 1960. Characteristics of Teacher Behavior Related to the Achievement of Children in Several Elementary Grades. Brooklyn College, Office of Testing and Research, Brooklyn, New York.

Hewett, F. M. 1967. "Educational Engineering with Emotionally Disturbed Children," Exceptional Child. 33(7):459-470, March.

Hinshelwood, James. 1917. Congenital Word-Blindness. H. K. Lewis, London.

Hirshberg, J. Cotter. 1953. "The Role of Education in the Treatment of Emotionally Disturbed Children Through Planned Ego Development," American Journal of Orthopsychiatry. 23:684-690.

Hobbs, N. 1965. How the Reed Plan Developed. In N. J. Long, W. C. Morse, and R. G. Newman (Eds.). Conflict in the Classroom. Wadsworth Publishing Co., Belmont, California.

Hollister, W. G., and S. E. Goldston. 1962. Considerations for Planning Classes for the Emotionally Handicapped. Council for Exceptional Children of the National Education Association, Washington, D.C. March.

Hymes, James L., Jr. 1949. Teacher Listen: The Children Speak. State Charities Aid Association, New York.

Hymes, James L., Jr. 1955. Behavior and Misbehavior. Prentice-Hall, Englewood Cliffs, New Jersey.

Jackson, J. Hughlings. 1932. Selected Writings of James Taylor (Ed.). Hodden and Stroughton, London.

Jacobson, Stanley, and Christopher Faegre. 1959. "Neutralization: A Tool for the Teacher of Disturbed Children," Exceptional Children. 25:243-246.

Knoblock, P., and R. A. Garcea. 1965. "Toward a Broader Concept of the Role of the Special Class for Emotionally Disturbed Children," Exceptional Child. 31:329. March.

Kuenzli, A. E. 1958. "Field Experience Program with Emotionally Disturbed Children," Exceptional Child. 25:158-161. December.

Lippman, Hyman S. 1956. Treatment of the Child in Emotional Conflict. McGraw-Hill Publishing Co., New York.

Mahler, Donald. 1964. Instructional Planning for Educationally Handi-
    capped Children. Orinda Union School District, Orinda, California.

Malmquist, Eve. 1958. Factors Related to Reading Disabilities in the
    First Grade of the Elementary School. Almquist and Wiksells,
    Stockholm, Sweden.

Mariner, A. S., E. Brandt, E. C. Stone, and E. L. Mirmow. 1961. "Group
    Psychiatric Consultation with Public School Personnel: A Two-
    Year Study," Personnel Guidance. 40:154-258.

Medley, Donald M., and Harold E. Mitzel. 1959. "Some Behavioral
    Correlates of Teacher Effectiveness," Journal of Educational
    Psychology. 50:239-246.

Miller, O. B., J. Young, and M. M. Lawrence. 1963. "A Mental Health
    Consultation Program," The National Elementary Principal. 42:45.

Money, John (Ed.). 1962. Reading Disability, Progress and Research
    Needs by Dyslexia. John Hopkins Press, Baltimore, Maryland.

Morse, W. C. 1962. "The Crisis Teacher, Public School Provision for the
    Disturbed Pupil," The University of Michigan School of Education
    Bulletin, 27:101-104. April.

Morse, W. C., R. L. Cutler, and A. H. Fink, 1964. Public School Classes
    for the Emotionally Handicapped: A Research Analysis. Univer-
    sity of Michigan Press, East Lansing, Michigan.

Moustakas, Clark E. 1953. Children in Play Therapy. McGraw-Hill Book
    Company, New York.

Moustakas, Clark E. 1956. The Teacher and the Child. McGraw-Hill
    Book Company, New York.

Mullen, F. A., and L. H. Blumenthal. 1962. "Principles of Agency-
    School Cooperation in a Program for Emotionally Disturbed Child-
    ren," American Journal of Orthopsychiatry. 32(1):109-118. January.

Nass, Martin L. 1959. "Characteristics of a Psychotherapeutically
    Oriented Group for Beginning Teachers," Mental Hygiene. 43:
    562-567.

Neill, A. S. 1960. Summerhill: A Radical Approach to Child Rearing.
    Hart Publishing Co., New York.

Newman, Ruth G. 1956. "The Acting-Out Boy," Exceptional Children. 22:

186-190, 204-216.

Newman, R. G., R. Redl, and H. Kitchner, 1965. Technical Assistance. In N. J. Long, W. C. Morse, and R. C. Newman (Eds.). Conflict in the Classroom. Wadsworth Publishing Co., Belmont, California.

Orton, Samuel T., M.D. 1928. "Specific Reading Disability-Strephosymbolia," The Journal of the American Medical Association. 90: 1095-1099. April 7.

Pearson, Gerald H. J. 1949. Emotional Disorders of Children. Norton and Co., New York.

Pearson, Gerald H. J. 1954. Psychoanalysis and the Education of the Child. Norton and Co., New York.

Phillips, E. Lakin. 1956. Psychotherapy: A Modern Theory and Practice. Prentice-Hall, Englewood Cliffs, New Jersey.

Phillips, E. Lakin. 1957a. "Contributions to a Learning Theory Account of Childhood Autism," Journal of Clinical Psychology. 43:117-124.

Phillips, E. Lakin. 1957b. "Some Features of Child Guidance Clinic Practice in the U.S.A.," Journal of Clinical Psychology. 13: 42-44.

Phillips, E. Lakin. 1957c. "The Problem of Motivation: Some Neglected Aspects," Journal of Rehabilitation. 23:10-12.

Phillips, E. Lakin. 1957d. "The Use of the Teacher as Adjunct Therapist in Child Guidance," Psychiatry. 20:407-410.

Phillips, E. Lakin. 1958a. "Experimental Results from Special Teaching Techniques for Emotionally Disturbed Children," paper presented to the American Association for the Advancement of Science, Washington, D.C., December 26.

Phillips, E. Lakin. 1958b. "New Approaches," in Daniel Brower and L.E. Abt (eds.). Progress in Clinical Psychology, Vol. 111. Grune and Stratton, New York.

Phillips, E. Lakin. 1959. "The Role of Structure in Psychotherapy," American Psychologist. 14:389. (Abstract).

Phillips, E. Lakin. 1960. "Parent-Child Psychotherapy: A Follow-up Study Comparing Two Techniques," Journal of Psychology. 49: 195-202.

Phillips, E. Lakin, and Norris G. Haring. 1959. "Results from Special Techniques for Teaching Emotionally Disturbed Children," Exceptional Children. 26:64-67.

Phillips, E. Lakin, and M.H.S. Johnston. 1954. "Theory and Development of Parent Child, Short-Term Psychotherapy," Psychiatry. 17: 267-275.

Phillips, E. Lakin, Daniel N. Wiener, and Norris G. Haring. 1960. Discipline, Achievement and Mental Health. Prentice-Hall Englewood Cliffs, New Jersey.

Prescott, Daniel A. 1938. Emotions and the Educative Process. American Council on Education, Washington, D. C.

Prescott, Daniel A. 1957. The Child in the Educative Process. McGraw-Hill Book Company, New York.

Redl, Fritz, and William W. Wattenberg. 1951. Mental Hygiene in Teaching. Harcourt, Brace, New York.

Redl, Fritz, and David Wineman. 1951. Children who Hate. Free Press, New York.

Redl, Fritz, and David Wineman. 1952. Controls from Within. Free Press, New York.

Reid, Joseph H., and Helen R. Gagan. 1952. Residential Treatment of Emotionally Disturbed Children. Child Welfare League of America, New York.

Richards, J. 1962-1963. "Teaching Used in a School Emerging from Early Infantile Autism," Exceptional Child. 29:348-357.

Robinson, Helen M. 1946. Why Pupils Fail in Reading. University of Chicago Press, Chicago, Illinois.

Rogers, Carl R. 1942. Counseling and Psychotherapy. Houghton Mifflin, Boston, Massachusetts.

Rogers, Carl R. 1951. Client-Centered Therapy. Houghton Mifflin, Boston, Massachusetts.

Rosen, S. N. 1960-61. A Method Dealing with Mental Health Problems. CEC Monograph.

Rosner, J. 1957. "Therapy with Latchkey Children," American Journal of

Orthopsychiatry. 27:411-419. April.

Simpson, Roy E. 1961. "The Education of Emotionally Handicapped
    Children," report prepared for the California State
    Department of Education, Sacramento, California.

Slavson, Samuel R. 1954. Re-educating the Delinquent Through Group
    and Community Participation. Harper, New York.

Smith, Donald E. P., and Patricia M. Carrigan. 1959. The Nature of
    Reading Disability. Harcourt, Brace, and Co., New York.

Sperry, R. W. 1964. "The Great Cerebral Commissure," Scientific
    American. 210-42-52. January.

Strauss, Alfred A., and Laura E. Lehtinen. 1947. Psychopathology and
    Education of the Brain-Injured Child, Vol. 1. Grune and
    Stratton, New York.

Strauss, Alfred A., and Newell C. Kephart. 1955. Psychopathology and
    Education of the Brain-Injured Child, Vol. 2. Grune and Stratton,
    New York.

Talmadge, M. 1963. "A Study of Experimental Methods for Teaching
    Emotionally Disturbed, Brain Damaged, Retarded Readers,"
    Journal of Educational Research. 56(6):311-315. February.

Weisenburg, Theodore, and Katharine E. McBride. 1935. Aphasia, A
    Clinical and Psychological Study. The Commonwealth Fund, New
    York.

Table 9. WRAT scores, Comparison Group

| Name | Grade | Age at Testing | Grade Placement | | | | | |
| | | | R | | S | | A | |
			Pre	Post	Pre	Post	Pre	Post
1C	3	8-3	1.4	2.1	1.0	1.8	1.9	2.5
2C	3	8-4	2.3	2.9	1.9	2.4	2.7	2.9
3C	3	8-1	1.9	2.7	1.5	2.2	1.9	2.3
4C	4	8-11	3.9	4.6	3.7	4.6	2.7	4.1
5C	3	9-3	2.9	3.2	2.3	2.5	2.5	2.6
6C	2	8-0	3.3	4.4	2.3	2.8	2.5	3.5

| Name | Grade | Age at Testing | Raw Score | | | | | |
| | | | R | | S | | A | |
			Pre	Post	Pre	Post	Pre	Post
1C	3	8-3	13	21	7	13	15	20
2C	3	8-4	25	29	14	19	21	22
3C	3	8-1	19	27	10	17	16	19
4C	4	8-11	39	44	32	37	6	14
5C	3	9-3	29	32	18	20	21	26
6C	2	8-0	33	44	18	23	20	25
Sum of Scores			158	197	99	129	99	126
Average			26.33	32.83	16.50	21.50	16.50	21.00

Average age at Testing: 8-5.67

Table 10. WRAT scores, Educo-Therapy Group

| | | | Grade Placement | | | | | |
| | | Age at | R | | S | | A | |
Name	Grade	Testing	Pre	Post	Pre	Post	Pre	Post
1E	3	8-11	2.1	2.4	1.6	2.2	2.5	2.6
2E	3	8-7	1.8	3.0	1.3	2.7	1.65	2.2
3E	2	7-1	3.5	4.4	2.1	3.8	2.3	2.7
4E	2	8-6	1.8	3.4	1.3	2.5	2.2	2.9
5E	3	9-1	2.9	3.5	1.8	2.9	2.3	3.9
6E	3	8-3	3.6	4.5	3.0	3.4	2.5	3.8

| | | | Raw Score | | | | | |
| | | Age at | R | | S | | A | |
Name	Grade	Testing	Pre	Post	Pre	Post	Pre	Post
1E	3	8-11	21	24	12	17	20	21
2E	3	8-7	18	30	9	22	13	18
3E	2	7-1	35	44	16	33	19	22
4E	2	8-6	18	34	9	20	18	22
5E	3	9-1	29	35	13	24	19	28
6E	3	8-3	36	45	25	29	20	27
Sum of Scores			157	212	84	145	109	138
Average			26.28	35.33	14.00	24.17	18.17	23.00

Average age at Testing: 8-5

Table 11. WRAT scores, Heterogeneous Group

Name	Grade	Age at Testing	Grade Placement R Pre	R Post	S Pre	S Post	A Pre	A Post
1H	3	8-2	2.2	2.7	2.0	2.0	2.5	2.5
2H	3	8-2	2.9	3.3	1.8	2.9	2.5	3.9
3H	3	9-3	4.5	7.5	2.5	3.4	2.5	3.1
4H	2	7-10	1.9	2.4	1.2	2.1	2.2	2.7
5H	2	7-11	.7	1.0	1.0	1.0	1.4	1.8
6H	3	8-1	5.3	6.0	3.8	5.1	3.3	4.4

Name	Grade	Age at Testing	Raw Score R Pre	R Post	S Pre	S Post	A Pre	A Post
1H	3	8-2	22	27	15	15	20	20
2H	3	8-2	29	33	13	30	20	28
3H	3	9-3	45	45	20	24	20	23
4H	2	7-10	19	24	8	23	18	21
5H	2	7-11	3	6	7	7	11	14
6H	3	8-1	53	69	33	40	24	31
Sum of Scores			171	194	96	139	113	137
Average			28.50	32.33	16.00	23.1	18.83	23.17

Average age at Testing: 8-2.8

65

Table 12. SRA scores (Raw scores), Comparison Group

Name	Grade	Comprehension		Vocabulary		Total Reading	
		Pre	Post	Pre	Post	Pre	Post
1C	2	6	12	8	12	7	135
2C	3	20	20	13	18	33	38
3C	2	15	16	12	10	27	26
4C	4	23	24	15	23	38	47
5C	3	22	18	9	13	31	31
6C	2	18	31	12	20	30	51
Sum of Scores		104	121	69	96		
Average		17.33	20.17	11.50	16.00		

Name	Grade	Cap. & Punc.		Gram. Usage		Spelling	
		Pre	Post	Pre	Post	Pre	Post
1C	2						
2C	3	20	30	15	20	5	7
3C	2	31	25	16	22	2	2
4C	4	50	50	33	35	19	20
5C	3	34	30	17	20	5	10
6C	2	35	41	14	29	6	9

(Table Continued)

Table 12. Continued

Name	Total Language Art		Concepts		Reasoning	
	Pre	Post	Pre	Post	Pre	Post
1C			13	18	10	26
2C	40	47	14	21	6	5
3C	49	49	11	15	4	7
4C	102	106	24	25	7	10
5C	56	60	13	23	8	4
6C	55	82	20	28	16	21
Sum of Scores			95	130	51	73
Average			15.83	21.67	8.50	12.00

Name	Computation		Total Arithmetic		Composite	
	Pre	Post	Pre	Post	Pre	Post
1C	17	5	40	49	137	184
2C	12	23	33	49	100	144
3C	4	6	19	28	95	103
4C	14	3	45	65	185	218
5C	12	22	33	49	120	140
6C	7	13	43	62	128	195
Sum of Scores	66	72	213	302	765	984
Average	11.00	12.00	35.50	50.35	127.50	164.00

Table 13. SRA scores (Raw scores), Educo-Therapy Group

Name	Grade	Comprehension		Vocabulary		Total Reading	
		Pre	Post	Pre	Post	Pre	Post
1E	2	19	18	15	14	139	155
2E	2	12	21	10	21	132	183
3E	2	23	31	22	26	45	57
4E	2	3	18	3	10	130	157
5E	3	21	36	16	28	37	64
6E	3	10	15	13	20		
Sum of Scores		88	136	79	119		
Average		14.67	22.67	13.17	19.83		

Name	Grade	Cap. & Punc.		Gram. Usage		Spelling	
		Pre	Post	Pre	Post	Pre	Post
1E	2						
2E	2						
3E	2	23	41	25	34	5	10
4E	2						
5E	3	33	42	27	32	5	5
6E	3	30	40	22	19	8	13

(Table Continued)

Table 13. Continued

Name	Total Language Arts		Concepts		Reasoning	
	Pre	Post	Pre	Post	Pre	Post
1E			17	31	18	35
2E			17	29	14	21
3E	53	85	11	26	7	15
4E			20	29	25	35
5E	65	84	23	31	15	19
6E	60	72	21	26	11	11
Sum of Scores			109	172	90	136
Average			18.17	28.67	15.00	22.67

Name	Computation		Total Arithmetic		Composite	
	Pre	Post	Pre	Post	Pre	Post
1E	25	21	60	87	199	242
2E	9	26	40	76	172	259
3E	6	15	24	56	122	198
4E	30	46	75	110	205	267
5E	13	18	51	68	153	216
6E	3	13	35	50	118	157
Sum of Scores	86	139	285	447	969	1339
Average	14.33	23.17	47.50	74.50	161.50	223.77

Table 14. SRA Scores (Raw scores), Heterogeneous Group

Name	Grade	Comprehension Pre	Comprehension Post	Vocabulary Pre	Vocabulary Post	Total Reading Pre	Total Reading Post
1H	2	15	16	7	9	22	25
2H	3	19	29	6	21	25	50
3H	3	29	35	24	29	53	64
4H	2	6	29	9	21	102	189
5H	2	10	13	8	14	71	117
6H	3	39	40	29	33	68	73
Sum of Scores		118	162	83	127		
Average		19.67	27.00	13.83	21.17		

Name	Grade	Cap. & Punc. Pre	Cap. & Punc. Post	Gram. Usage Pre	Gram. Usage Post	Spelling Pre	Spelling Post
1H	2	33	29	26	26	3	7
2H	3	35	49	20	31	3	9
3H	3	44	44	28	40	7	12
4H	2						
5H	2						
6H	3	43	49	40	40	15	21

(Table Continued)

70

Table 14. Continued.

Name	Total Language Arts		Concepts		Reasoning	
	Pre	Post	Pre	Post	Pre	Post
1H	62	62	17	20	10	10
2H	58	89	14	29	9	16
3H	79	90	24	27	14	15
4H			23	37	16	43
5H			10	19	10	22
6H	98	110	31	37	23	25
Sum of Scores			119	169	82	131
Average			19.83	28.17	13.67	21.83

Name	Computation		Total Arithmetic		Composite	
	Pre	Post	Pre	Post	Pre	Post
1H	11	15	38	45	122	127
2H	8	43	31	88	114	227
3H	10	15	48	57	156	211
4H	24	42	63	122	165	311
5H	0	7	20	48	91	165
6H	18	34	72	96	238	279
Sum of Scores	71	156	272	456	886	1320
Average	11.83	16.00	45.33	76.00	147.67	220.00

Table 15. WISC scores, pre-post differences[a]

	Comparison Group				Educo-Therapy Group		
	Edi	Needed	P		Edi	Needed	P
V.S.	0	+28	N.S.		+ 3	+ 9	N.S.
P.S.	+61	+51	Sig.		+36	+35	Sig.
F.S.	+31	+29	Sig.		+20	+22	N.S.
Info.	+ 2	+ 5	N.S.		+ 1	+ 1	Sig.
Comp.	-16	+10	N.S.		-16	+12	N.S.
Arith.	- 8	+10	N.S.		- 3	+ 6	N.S.
Sim.	+ 8	+ 6	Sig.		+18	+12	Sig.
Vocab.	- 6	+10	N.S.		+ 5	+ 7	N.S.
D. Sp.	+ 5	+ 5	Sig.		- 2	+ 4	N.S.
P.C.	+ 2	+ 4	N.S.		+ 9	+11	N.S.
P.A.	+23	+13	Sig.		+ 6	+10	N.S.
B.D.	+10	+ 6	Sig.		+ 9	+ 3	Sig.
O.A.	- 2	+ 6	N.S.		0	+ 2	N.S.
Coding	+ 7	+ 5	Sig.		+ 7	+ 9	N.S.

	Heterogeneous Group		
	Edi	Needed	P
V.S.	+18	+30	N.S.
P.S.	+14	+22	N.S.
F.S.	+2-	+2-	Sig.
Info.	- 5	+ 5	N.S.
Comp.	- 1	+13	N.S.
Arith.	+ 1	+13	N.S.
Sim.	+ 9	+11	N.S.
Vocab.	- 3	+ 5	N.S.
D. Sp.	+ 5	+ 7	N.S.
P.C.	- 1	+ 2	N.S.
P.A.	+ 6	+ 4	N.S.
B.D.	0	+ 4	N.S.
O.A.	+10	+ 6	Sig.
Coding	- 2	+ 8	N.S.

[a]Statistical Treatment: Randomization Test for Matched Pairs. Value presented in "Needed" column is lowest of three most extreme possible positive outcomes of that matched pair. If value obtained exceeds this, significance is reached.

Table 16. WRAT scores[a]

| | Comparison Group | | | Educo-Therapy Group | | |
	Edi	Needed	P	Edi	Needed	P
Reasoning	+39	+31	N.S.	+55	+43	Sig.
Arithmetic	+17	+15	Sig.	+61	+51	Sig.
Spelling	+27	+21	Sig.	+29	+23	Sig.

| | Heterogeneous Group | | |
	Edi	Needed	P
Reasoning	+23	+15	Sig.
Arithmetic	+43	+29	Sig.
Spelling	+24	+12	Sig.

[a]Statistical Treatment: Randomization Test for Matched Pairs. Value presented in "Needed" column is lowest of three most extreme possible positive outcomes of that matched pair. If value obtained exceeds this, significance is reached.

Table 17. SRA scores[a]

	Comparison Group				Educo-Therapy Group		
	Edi	Needed	P		Edi	Needed	P
Comprehension	+17	+21	N.S.		+51	+43	Sig.
Vocabulary	+27	+19	Sig.		+40	+34	Sig.
Total Reading	+72	+72	Sig.		+145	+113	Sig.
Cap. & Punc.	+ 9	+21	N.S.		+37	+37	Sig.
Grammar	+32	+26	Sig.		+11	+17	N.S.
Spelling	+11	+ 9	Sig.		+10	+10	Sig.
Total Language							
Art	+52	+44	Sig.		+63	+63	Sig.
Concepts	+35	+23	Sig.		+63	+63	Sig.
Reasoning	+24	+26	N.S.		+46	+32	Sig.
Computation	+ 6	+40	N.S.		+53	+47	Sig.
Total Arith.	+89	+57	Sig.		+147	+113	Sig.

	Heterogeneous Group		
	Edi	Needed	P
Comprehension	+54	+50	Sig.
Vocabulary	+44	+32	Sig.
Total Reading	+117	+107	Sig.
Cap. & Punc.	+17	+25	N.S.
Grammar	+17	+17	Sig.
Spelling	+21	+21	Sig.
Total Language			
Art	+54	+54	Sig.
Concepts	+54	+38	Sig.
Reasoning	+49	+45	Sig.
Computation	+98	+84	Sig.
Total Arithmetic	+184	+166	Sig.
Composite	+434	+354	Sig.

[a]Statistical Treatment: Randomization Test for Matched Pairs. Value presented in "Needed" column is lowest of three most extreme possible positive outcomes of that matched pair. If value obtained exceeds this, significance is reached.

Table 18. Process for in-school screening of children with emotional handicaps.

Name	Picture Game[a]		Behavioral Data Thinking About Yourself[b]		Class Play[c]	
	Pre	Post	Pre	Post	Pre	Post
Comparison Group						
1C	32	33↑	24	40	3	48↑
2C	18	24↑	28	56	17	7↓
3C	32	30↓	35	56	20	37↑
4C	20	30↑	17	38	23	33↑
5C	26	26+	37	50	10	20↑
6C	25	38↑	28	41	7	55↑
Sum of Scores	153	181	169	281	80	200
Average	25.50	30.17	28.17	46.83	13.33	33.33
Educo-Therapy Group						
1E	26	25↓	15	23↑	50	10↓
2E	43	32↓	40	14↓	50	23↓
3E	27	26↓	49	69↑	30	30+
4E	24	23↓	30	45↑	10	57↑
5E	27	32↑	43	53↑	40	77↑
6E	37	33↓	47	48↑	66	79↑
Sum of Scores	184	171	224	252	246	276
Average	30.67	28.50	37.33	42.00	41.00	46.00

(Table Continued)

Table 18. Continued

<table>
<tr><td rowspan="3">Name</td><td colspan="6" align="center">Behavioral Data
Thinking About</td></tr>
<tr><td colspan="2" align="center">Picture Game[a]</td><td colspan="2" align="center">Yourself[b]</td><td colspan="2" align="center">Class Play[c]</td></tr>
<tr><td>Pre</td><td>Post</td><td>Pre</td><td>Post</td><td>Pre</td><td>Post</td></tr>
<tr><td colspan="7">Heterogeneous Group</td></tr>
<tr><td>1H</td><td>24</td><td>38↑</td><td>15</td><td>31↑</td><td>33</td><td>13↓</td></tr>
<tr><td>2H</td><td>20</td><td>40↑</td><td>44</td><td>40↓</td><td>13</td><td>10↓</td></tr>
<tr><td>3H</td><td>19</td><td>30↑</td><td>47</td><td>31↓</td><td>20</td><td>13↓</td></tr>
<tr><td>4H</td><td>16</td><td>32↑</td><td>44</td><td>58↑</td><td>27</td><td>7↓</td></tr>
<tr><td>5H</td><td>47</td><td>24↓</td><td>19</td><td>31↑</td><td>43</td><td>0↓</td></tr>
<tr><td>6H</td><td>36</td><td>36↑</td><td>27</td><td>40↑</td><td>0</td><td>0·</td></tr>
<tr><td>Sum of Scores</td><td>162</td><td>200</td><td>196</td><td>228</td><td>136</td><td>43</td></tr>
<tr><td>Average</td><td>27.00</td><td>33.33</td><td>32.67</td><td>38.00</td><td>22.67</td><td>7.17</td></tr>
</table>

[a]Research shows that pupils with very high scores (many happy pictures) often have as many emotional problems as pupils with very low scores (few happy pictures). Scores below 20 or above 37 are indicators of emotional disturbance.

[b]A low score on "Thinking About Yourself" indicates that a pupil's ideal self and perceived self are very much the same. A high score indicates that a pupil sees himself quite differently from what he would like to be.

[c]High percentage indicates student identified with negative role and also that the student perceives teachers and classmates selecting him for negative roles.

Table 19. Process for in-school screening of children with emotional handicaps.[a]

	Comparison Group			Educo-Therapy Group		
	Edi	Needed	P	Edi	Needed	P
Picture Game	+27	+21	Sig.	-14	+20	N.S.
Thinking About Yourself	+124	+92	Sig.	+32	+64	N.S.
Class Play	+120	-106	N.S.	+30	-100	N.S.

	Heterogeneous Group		
	Edi	Needed	P
Picture Game	+38	+56	N.S.
Thinking About Yourself	-15	+47	N.S.
Class Play	-73	-59	Sig.

[a]Statistical Treatment: Randomization Test for Matched Pairs. Value presented in "Needed" column is lowest of three most extreme possible positive outcomes of that matched pair. If value obtained exceeds this, significance is reached.

Table 20. Bender Gestalt scores

Educo-Therapy Group		Heterogeneous Group			
Pre	Post	Pre	Post		
83	55	65	50	89	
61	49	125	114	54	
150	99		70	139	
138	113		76	79	
99	86	77	80	82	
130	79		80	107	72
631	481	521	470	550	420

Mean

105	80	87	78	92	70

Mean Change

-25	-13	-22

Table 21. Bender Gestalt scores[a]

		Two Tailed Test	
	Need	Obtained	P
Educo (pre-post)	181	-181	.05
Hetero (pre-post)	53	- 50	N.S.
Comparison (pre-post)	136	-130	N.S.

[a]Statistical Treatment: Randomization Test. Test of significance of difference between two related samples.